Author: Nabeel Zaidi, LLB (Hons), LLM, PG. Dip., DMS, Cert. Ed., MBA, Barrister

I0484760

About this publication

This is an essay about Jeremy Bentham's Auto-Icon, which is represented by a pamphlet outlining his desire to be dissected for medical experimentation after his demise and also the public display of his physical remains in the Cloisters building at University College London. The essay considers the context, motivation and rationale for adopting such a radical stance for its time. The essay included research of Bentham's unpublished manuscripts and published works. The essay formed part of an LLM Master's degree in Law at University College London during 1995-1996 (and was awarded a 'Distinction'). It may prove useful to individuals reading law, history, philosophy, sociology or those with a general interest in Jeremy Bentham and, unlike many other publications in this genre, can be read in one sitting.

1

photocopying, recording, or otherwise, without the prior permission of the copyright owner of this book.

ISBN-13: 978-1511570992

ISBN-10: 1511570997

Contents

Jeremy Bentham's Auto-Icon: an egoistic advertisement for reform

> "A philosopher's last thoughts are usually of some interest; in the case of Bentham they are so surprisingly like the whole tenor of his life that they deserve some exploration" (Fenn; 1992: iii)

1. Introduction

The "Auto-Icon" is situated in a secluded corner of the South Cloisters building at University College London, clothing the preserved bones and wax head[1] of Jeremy Bentham, open daily for display, providing the uninitiated

---

[1] The original preserved and fluid-drained head is kept in the UCL vaults.

observer with little insight into the life of the social reformer, the utilitarian and the empirical sceptic.

The "Auto-Icon" also refers to an unpublished pamphlet, written just before Bentham's death, encompassing implicit references and links to most of his life's work and providing, in combination with his wish to be dissected, an indication (which until recently has not been publicly discussed) as to his motivations for adopting such a radical position for his time.

This is not to say that authoritative and thought provoking books and articles have not been published on this area, but what has been published has, however, been predominantly concerned with locating these two aspects within a medical-history standpoint[1] examining in particular the attitudes towards dissection, omitting discussion or analysis of the variety of Bentham's other works, which provide some persuasive causal links for his position on dissection and iconisation.

The aim of this essay, then, which is divided into three parts: (dissection, auto-icon, and egoism), is to locate Bentham's auto-icon within his broader lifetime's publications, extracting as we proceed the motivations which led him to request his dissection and iconisation. Such a discussion should provide a much needed gloss on both these aspects of his life - transcending the ridicule that his auto-icon has generated amongst some

---

[1] Ruth Richardson's publications have proved to be both thorough and invaluable in this respect, providing the much needed historical and, to some extent, political background to dissection.

commentators to reveal a consistent and rational (although somewhat egoistic) reformer.

Consistency provided the 'back bone' to Bentham's empiricism and this is reflected also in his position on dissection, which he maintained till the end, stating that "[b]y [dissection] I shall have made to the fund of human happiness a contribution, more or less considerable" (Fenn; 1992: 2). It is to this discussion that I now turn.

2. Regulating dissection

In the early nineteenth century the gallows provided the only source of corpses for anatomists to dissect, with the act of dissection representing a means of punishment, denying a Christian burial to those hanged and leading to increased hostility and local tension amongst the dissected victim's family and friends.

Coupled with an increase in demand for more effective medical practice (particularly by the affluent), this militated an expanding black market in body snatching, satiating such demand but only at a significant profit, thus ensuring that no individuals' buried remains were beyond pillage. The emergence, however, of new security-conscious coffins and guarding facilities pioneered by entrepreneurs, to a large extent, increased the risk of appropriation for those not in a position to make the arrangements for such protection on death (in particular the indigent poor).

At this point it may be argued that Bentham was himself concerned to avoid being exhumed for dissection upon burial, but this argument is weakened by the fact that he bequeathed his body in 1769, at the age of 21, in a will deposited in the hands of Chamberlain Richard Clark an Attorney at law. In the absence of evidence to suggest that Bentham's health was failing during this period in his life, it is more convincing to suggest that this was the adoption of a moral and empirical stance in opposition to the church, which endorsed Christian burial and disapproved of dissection.[1]

Moreover, Bentham by the time of his death had inherited a considerable legacy and consequently was a man of some financial standing. Given the new, although not fool-proof, security measures for the dead available at that time, together with the likely passage of the Anatomy Act[2], it is difficult to accept the fear of exhumation for dissection as a strong motivational factor leading Bentham to adopt the position that he did, despite the growing activity amongst the body snatchers.[3]

The body snatchers bore the brunt of popular disdain for securing the supply of bodies for dissection, galvanising the anatomists from blame for maintaining the demand for such illegal activity. It was not until 1827-8 that a change in the case law led to the conviction of an anatomist,

---

[1] As Richardson (1988: 80) observes " ... Christian sentiment endorsed the need for permitting the natural decay of the integral body, and for its protection during the process."

[2] Bentham died on 6 June 1832, while the Anatomy Bill was between its first and second readings in the Lords (Richardson; 1987:3).

[3] It must be noted, however, that "Bentham must have been aware that his body would have been a prize specimen in any anatomical or phonological museum" (Richardson; 1987: 7).

prompting parliamentary activity in developing legal regulation of any future supply of bodies for dissection, which was concordant with long held demands by the medical profession for legal reform.

To this end, Bentham's draft bill (entitled "A Bill for the more effectual prevention of the violation of Burial Places"), which was contained in a correspondence to Robert Peel two years earlier, had a profound influence on the Anatomy Act, attracting Benthamite sympathisers at key levels, leading some to suggest that the Select Committee on Anatomy (responsible for conducting investigations and gathering evidence for the Act) favoured their views (Richardson; 1988:108).

Bentham's draft bill recommended the legal recognition of an implied contract between patient and charity/hospital so that in the event of death, in return for medical care, the patient's corpse would be at the disposal of the hospital's dissectors. This was with the proviso that if surviving relatives swore to their relationship within 24 hours of the death the body would be delivered to them for burial without dissection.

However, where there were 'extraordinary symptoms' a post-mortem would be carried out to determine the cause of death, with £100 being paid to the relatives in cases where the body was not subsequently returned to them. In addition to which, the draft bill proposed a Christian burial for the dissected remains at the anatomist's cost, the use of administrators in keeping dissection records and newspaper publication of the names of the deceased, and a repeal of the Act under which murderers were dissected (Richardson; 1986:26-7).

Curiously enough, Bentham's draft bill did not address itself to the need to establish an Inspectorate of Anatomy to oversee and enforce the Act, leaving aside also the potential conflict concerning the supply of dead bodies for dissection between the 'independent' private schools of anatomy and the schools attached to hospitals which yielded income to top surgeons. Notwithstanding these deficiencies, the Act, while adopting some of Bentham's proposals, such as abolishing the use of dissection as a method of punishment for murder, was not faithful to his draft bill either in content or in enforcement, omitting to include most of his proposals.

Moreover, the Act did not prohibit grave-robbery[1], providing no additional deterrent for this activity than available to the courts from pre-existing case law, with the number and powers of Anatomy Inspectors proving to be inadequate for the purposes of enforcing the Act (Richardson; 1988:209).

In combination with the Poor Law reforms, the Anatomy Act augmented the "systematic dismantling of older and more humanitarian methods of perceiving and dealing with poverty" (Richardson 1988:206), for while the Poor Law reforms exploited the indigent poor's labour at a profit (for those owning and managing the panopticon poor houses), with the eventual aim to lower the poor rates and maintain social order, the Anatomy Act could be interpreted as

---

[1] This may have been a tactical decision, initially ensuring that the supply of bodies to the anatomists would not be suddenly curtailed.

having had a dual effect. First, it potentially exploited the remains of the indigent poor for a profit (whether financial or in the form of enhanced medical knowledge) and, secondly, it displaced disquiet about dissection present amongst the middle-classes, who had growing influence in society.

Subsequent years, however, saw a number of amendments to the Act, which are discussed at some length by Richardson (1988), along with the historical influences impacting on them. Indeed, the socio-political and legal climate has changed since Bentham's time and so in relating his work to dissection the discussion will be located in a historical setting in order to reveal his reformist and, to some extent, radical standpoint. It is to Bentham's wider legal and political thought and work that I now turn, identifying the influences leading him to favour dissection and the content of his draft bill.

As mentioned earlier, Bentham's discourse has reflected a consistent scepticism, commencing, as far as we know, in 1760, when at the age of twelve he entered Queen's College Oxford, at which point his religious scepticism manifested itself in a reluctance to subscribe to the 39 Articles of the Church of England. But it was the works of 'Enlightenment' writers such as Locke, Montesquieu, Helvetius, Becarria, Newton and Bacon that formed the foundation of Bentham's empiricism, being reflected in his principle of utility, espousing the minimisation of pain, the maximisation of pleasure, and the 'greatest happiness of the greatest number'.

For Bentham, dissection was the finale to a lifetime's empiricism maintaining his assertion that we should be guided by the twin empirical standards of pain and pleasure, which were firmly located in our life on earth and which were no longer realisable, at least not in the absence of proof to the contrary, after our demise. A logical progression from this point, and one which Bentham acceded to, was to posit that dissection caused no empirically demonstrable pain for the victim, while also maximising the happiness of mankind through the augmentation of human medical knowledge, thus justifying it.

Nevertheless, Bentham was sensitive to the strong religious objections that dissection attracted amongst a cross-section of the population; but in realising the importance of dissection for the furtherance of mankind he provided a compromise[1] within his draft bill, making a useful distinction between *post-mortem* and *dissection,* with the former being compulsory in cases involving 'extraordinary symptoms', while the latter provided a slightly more flexible approach, allowing a relative to claim the body within 24 hours to avoid dissection.[2]

---

[1] Throughout Bentham's public proposals for reform, such as the Poor Law reforms, the Panopticon, etc., he recognised the conservative nature of his audience and consequently diluted some of his reform proposals to make them more acceptable, ensuring in effect that his audience was not alienated.

[2] This period, given the slow communication and transport facilities of that period, was too short to recover the body without dissection, thus leading one to the conclusion that this provision was loaded towards dissection.

This compromising nature may well have masked Bentham's true standpoint, something which is evident in at least one aspect of the dissection debate, that relating to people's Christian beliefs and superstitions. The main resistance was certainly based on such grounds, with the church doing little to revise this position, maintaining its insistence on Christian burials, demonstrating, as it did in his other works, that the power of the church would prove to be a serious impediment to reform and thus forming a target for Bentham's numerous direct and indirect attacks on its authority.

To this extent, dissection can, for Bentham, be conceptualised as an act of defiance against the church. This does not, however, entail an atheist stance for him, but rather, an agnostic one, for nowhere in his work does he reject the existence of a divine being.[1] In fact, to do so would be to weaken his empirical position, for while he could not prove the existence of such a being, he could not, by the same token, categorically disprove it. Instead, it was the sinister interest, usually found in unquestioned authority, which concerned him. In relation to dissection, it was the fear of such interest manifesting itself (particularly in the body-snatchers and the anatomists) through the unregulated supply of dead bodies for dissection that may have prompted him to call for legal regulation of dissection[2]

---

[1] See further: Berman (1990:192)

[2] Alternatively, one could assert that as Bentham's lifetime was spent in studying the 'art' of legislation - coupled with his mistrust of the common law , and his command-based theory of sovereignty - that his call for reform necessitated a statute-based response.

Moreover, it was the maintenance of 'security' that formed the core of Bentham's enterprise, for without it law itself could not be represented in a viable and stable form, or at least not in Bentham's terms. Security here referred to life, property and expectation, and it was the role of government to ensure that these were maintained. Security of expectation was given a high utility value by Bentham as it provided certainty and stability.

If security was to be maintained in the long-run then there needed to be some form of redistribution to the indigent poor, ensuring that they did not invade the security of others, a situation which may have been more harmful in the future than redistribution now (Quinn; 1994:81-96). This may at first sight appear to conflict with Bentham ' s conservative approach to security, but closer examination, particularly of his work *Supply Without Burthen* (in Waldron; 1987) suggests that, when faced with insecurity in the long-run, short-run security can to some extent be forfeited. In the panopticon poor house proposals, however, Bentham effectively 'squared the circle' by making the indigent poor labour to support themselves, thus overcoming invasion of security, even in the short-run.[1]

While this analysis cannot be imported wholesale into the legal regulation of dissection debate, its tenor remains persuasive, for it was the indigent poor that suffered the disproportionate impact of body snatching, with this class

---

[1] One problem with this approach, however, is that it does not take in to account the displacement effect that they would have when released into the domestic labour market, particularly when considering their training and conditioning for hard work.

also disproportionately represented on the gallows, and although the growing unrest amongst the indigent poor certainly posed a threat to the maintenance of security it was an insubstantial one, but one nevertheless. Bentham's draft bill would, as it stood, probably have abated such a threat, but in the process of doing so, encroached upon the initial security of the anatomists by potentially reducing their unregulated supply of dead bodies for dissection. It may, on the other hand, have reduced the relative cost of the regulated supply.[1]

In any case, this appears to have been alleviated in two respects, first, by the implied contract with the patient and charity/hospital to perform dissection if the individual died while receiving medical care and, secondly, by providing such a short time limit (24 hours) in which relatives could claim the bodies of the deceased in order to avoid dissection.

If, as the draft bill suggested, the dissection provision was in return for medical treatment of the subsequently deceased patient then it appears to have been *prima facie* a consensual relationship, but the reality is one of economic coercion, for the only other option open to the indigent poor was to forego such treatment and risk the possibility of death anyway. Coupled with this was the potential spectre of disquiet amongst the family and friends of the deceased who, having not been claimed within 24 hours due to whatever reason - had been dissected. Bentham may have anticipated this when he inserted the requirement that a Christian burial be

---

[1] This could be because supply would be made more consistent, with no adverse manipulation and restriction imposed by body snatchers.

awarded to those dissected at the anatomist's expense, thus possibly reducing their exposure to such public disquiet.[1]

Furthermore, Bentham's mistrust of unquestioned authority (in this case, the potential power that the anatomists held) and the importance attached to the principles of contract management probably led him to advocate a £100 fine for those bodies which had post-mortems performed on them but not returned to the relatives (thus suggesting their misdirection for dissection).

Contract management provided a financial check and balance on the administrator (anatomist). In the proposed panopticon prison the governor's remuneration would have been diminished per dead prisoner over and above the average calculated mortality rate. To an analogous extent the "life assurance" principle in the panopticon poorhouse proposals guaranteed the health and life of inmates so that a diminution in either of these would have adversely affected the administrator's fee.

Bentham went one step further, requiring dissection records to be kept, together with publication of the deceased's name, making them readily available for public scrutiny. The influence for this may be seen to emanate from the "Public Opinion Tribunal", developed in his *Constitutional Code,* representing a useful fictitious entity comprising of, and dependent upon, the scrutiny and

---

[1] This may have been particularly true for those indigent poor who would not otherwise have been able to afford either medical treatment or a Christian burial.

moral censure of the public at large in order to be effective.[1]

The public's approval of the functionary's /anatomist's actions would provide a moral reward - perhaps in the form of co-operation by the public - which would be of benefit to the functionary. Conversely, where sinister interests were prevalent the reverse would be true (Schofield; 1991-2: 54-5). This for Bentham provided an important (moral) sanction - as effective as others - and one which should, with other administrative and legally enforceable mechanisms, ensure Compliance.[2]

The sanction of punishment for Bentham was the infliction of pain, the concomitant being that punishment required a live victim and consequently, post-death dissection could not, at least not in an empirical sense, be viewed as 'punishment'. To assert that it could, created a useless fiction mystifying and distorting positive law.

Post-death punishment could only be related to a form of moral censure, based not on a 'viable' standard but on one which was parasitic to Christian (particularly church-led) beliefs and superstitions, factors which may well have been at the forefront of Bentham's mind (in addition to maintaining security) when he proposed the abolition of dissection for murderers' corpses.

---

[1] The 'public' were not limited by physical boundaries but included "the inhabitants not only of the territory of the political state in question, but every other territory on the earth's surface" *(First Principles* p57)
[2] Similar contemporary arguments are forthcoming in relation to open government and freedom of information, which are viewed as serious and increasingly necessary government.

Bentham's vision of dissection was a serious attempt to augment the scientific, rational and empirical approach to changing both society's norms and laws, ensuring that the happiness of mankind was maximised. Conversely, his views tended to vary somewhat in relation to iconisation, with some overlap existing between it and dissection. For instance, while Bentham advocated bodily dissection, he did not include the human head within this, a reason perhaps being that it possessed some sacred quality or that its preservation would maintain a physical memory of the deceased individual.

A sympathetic interpretation may, however, be drawn from the distinction he created between corruptible and incorruptible human parts: "the mass of matter which death has created, [should] be disposed of with a view to the felicity of mankind - in a word, to the best advantage - the comparatively incorruptible part converted into an Auto-Icon - the soft and corruptible parts employed for the purpose of anatomical instruction, in so far as there is a demand for them" (Fenn; 1992: 3). The issue of dissection pre-empts, to some extent, Bentham's view on "Auto-Iconism", which is divided into two sections, the first, dealing with, what some interpret as the serious topic of dissection, while the second has tended to be interpreted as the less serious matter of auto-icons.

The discussion will now focus on the "Auto-Icon" pamphlet, commencing with an examination of dissection and auto-icon status, followed by an exposition of the many links that are contained within it which have either not already been analysed in the above discussion or not done so in relation to the auto-icon. The main aim of this analysis is to provide a thorough examination, attempting to reveal the true intentions of the pamphlet which have not as yet been appreciated by both those that have read and passed comment on it and those who have chosen to ignore it.

3. Re-reading the Auto-Icon

The "Auto-Icon" is a term which, like many others, was created by Bentham (Fenn 1992: 2) and is defined by the use of a technique developed further by him called paraphrasis[1]: "The word *auto* has been made familiar to English ears by its use in auto biography (why should there not be *auto-thanatography?), autograph,* etc. *Auto-Icon* will soon be understood for a man who is his own image" (Fenn; 1992:4).

There are a number of reasons for adopting iconisation, the most explicit of which is detailed in the pamphlet in rather verbose language (as Bentham had become accustomed to in his later years and for which he received criticism[2] and provides a link with our earlier discussion on

---

[1] By 'paraphrasis' a fiction is explained by being employed in a sentence or proposition, which is then translated into another sentence the words of which "are expressive of such ideas as are *simple,* or more immediately resolvable into simple ones than those of the former" *(A Fragment on Government* 495n) .

[2] The criticism which he received was mainly directed at the apparent contradiction in his work between his aim of clarifying the language of law, making it more accessible to the average person and the reality of

dissection. As he stated "But why, it may be asked, should more attention be paid to the senseless carcuss of the biped [(man)], than to that of the quadruped [(animal probably domestic, given the nature of the discussion)]? Because, if human carcusses are saleable, their value is a motive to murder. The pecuniary value attached to them created murderers in the shape of Burkes and Hares"[1] (Fenn; 1992:11).

This concern was linked with the legal regulation of supplying dead bodies to the anatomists for dissection. An auto-icon would, to some extent, have ensured that dead bodies were not snatched because they would have lost their medical usefulness. Alternatively, and this was perhaps Bentham's underlying intention, if one is willing to be mounted after death then an individual may well agree to be dissected first, the eventual aim being to diminish the preoccupation and superstition with burial, particularly Christian church-led burial.[2]

Unregulated supply of bodies for dissection probably also led him to argue for property rights in an auto-icon, thus effecting some legal penalty for misappropriating a deceased's body (Fenn; 1992:167). Property rights were also a means of providing security of expectation, ensuring a greater likelihood of reducing bodysnatching, and a

---

the verbose and unclear language used predominantly in his last works.

[1] Burke and Hare were notorious murderers, providing medical schools with anatomical specimens to order.

[2] A mounting problem of that time was the over-crowding of churchyards and the relatively high burial charges which impacted disproportionately on the indigent poor.

means of legal recourse to recover the remains and prosecute the assailants.

Indeed, as Kelly (1989:68) points out, security of property was fundamental to Bentham's theory, for it was one of the most important sources of individual well-being , and while it was not, and could not have been, an absolute principle for Bentham (see earlier), it would have provided protection for a deceased's body, incorporating stringent property rights enforceable at law.

Such a formulation appears to be coherent and persuasive, at least in theory, yet the practicalities of enforcing these 'property rights' were contingent upon comprehensive legal regulation, enforcement techniques and, most importantly, a high detection rate. Given the inherent limitations of technological and financial resources in Bentham's time to identify dead bodies efficiently, particularly if they were supplied in parts, effective detection could not have been possible, thus minimising any deterrent effect that regulation of this kind could engender.

Another reason for an auto-icon and one which provided a three part benefit to society was predicated on medical grounds; first, "it would obviate danger to health from the acumulation of putrid bodies"; second, "it would serve to dissipate the prejudice and delusion which object to dissection"; and finally, "it would furnish the most commodious and perfect representation of the difference between the heads of the inhabitants of different parts of the globe ... and comparison with those of clever animals, as the ape, the dog etc." (Fenn; 1992:12)

The inappropriate and overcrowded burial provision for the majority of the indigenous poor threatened the rest of society with the risk of disease (such as cholera). Dissection followed by iconisation may have minimised the risk of disease and overcrowding, but more to the point, burial served little useful purpose for Bentham, particularly when medical science was thirsting for knowledge and held the potential for the furtherance of the welfare of mankind. The burial of individuals underground, left to decompose slowly, served little scientific or useful purpose, according to Bentham.

In fact, funeral expenses were high and impacted disproportionately on the indigenous poor. For Bentham, such an expense "had the effect of a tax" on the surviving family members or relatives of the deceased (*Ibid.* 1992:14). More seriously for him, it represented a tax on, and even confiscation of, property in order to finance funeral expenses. This inevitably undermined security of possession of the indigent poor, making them, at best, even more incumbent upon the charity of others and, at worst, a threat to the security of possession of others.

Unlike today, the mortality rate of the indigent poor in Bentham's time was high and consequently families increased procreation to counteract this, thus compounding the burden of funeral expenses in the long-run. However, like today, funeral expenses were disproportionately high, with death providing a healthy profit for the funeral services (and, in Bentham's time, for the church).

From a Benthamite perspective, burial expenses reduced the 'happiness' of the indigent poor, particularly when such funerals were over-lavish for the payer's means (*Ibid.* 1992:15). Moreover, iconisation would have maximised value and minimised expense, with value being maximised by removal of 'burdens' such as burial costs (thus also minimising expense) and facilitating enjoyment and 'instruments' of enjoyment (Fenn; 1992:14) providing a physical representation of the deceased, whose memory they could maintain more vividly.

There were many uses to which the auto-icon could be put. Amongst these was to use it as a form of monument to the dead (*Ibid.* 1992:6), being displayed in churches (*Ibid.* 1992:4) or family dwellings (*Ibid.* 1992:5) , being exhibited "and their exhibition associated with religious observances" and accompanied by music[1] (*Ibid.* 1992:5).

There would also have been a form of punishment for auto-icons of criminals administered by public opinion, with those whom the public still had not forgiven to be placed in a 'temple of dishonour' until such a time that public opinion changed as a result of being "enlightened by experience, by knowledge, by philosophy". In the meantime, those auto-icons which had been wrongly dishonoured would be transported to the 'temple of honour' (*Ibid.* 1992:10), while those who the public did not consider to have led a 'good life'[2] would have the head of their auto-icon reversed.

---

[1] Music was one of Bentham's prized recreational pursuits.
[2] What is meant by a 'good life' would be left to the public to interpret.

The uses to which the auto-icon was to be put indicates a humorous attack on the church - a means of reducing its standing and influence in the community and echoing a similar sentiment to that in the poor law reform proposals, where churches were to be used as banks for the poor to deposit and withdraw their remuneration.[1] The notion of punishing the auto-icon of a criminal may appear to be ridiculous, but no more so than punishing a hanged criminal by dissection. It is precisely this use of satire which has not been analysed further by other commentators.

Turning to the few commentators who have briefly written about the auto-icon pamphlet, one will find that they have provided a rather unsympathetic account of it[2] believing it to be, in the main, an anti-religious statement (Crimmins; 1990:298), thus providing a narrow interpretation[3] of Bentham's position on religion. One such interpretation, not as authoritative as it might at first sight appear, is provided by Crimmins (1990:296), who depicts Bentham as an "atheist and rigorous utilitarian", as showing the "irrelevance of religion" and pursuing a utilitarian society. It is difficult to find consistent authority to lend weight to such assertions.

---

[1] In the auto-icon pamphlet Bentham again had another function for the church: there would be a lecture room providing tuition on subjects for "anatomical-moral" instruction, together with the exhibition of auto-icons.

[2] See Fenn (1992:iii-vii), and Crimmins (1990:298-307)

[3] By a 'narrow interpretation' I mean that little has been said concerning the many components and links found in the pamphlet, together with the distinction between the church and religion per se, which are viewed slightly differently by Bentham, but which Crimmins, for example, does not discuss.

At the surface of Bentham's writings on religion there may be particular passages to cling to, supporting Crimmin's interpretation, but a careful reading, in view of the force of Bentham's other works, should reveal, as with Shakespeare's works, intricate 'sub-plots', importing other criticisms and agendas Bentham has, illustrations of which are provided in the earlier discussion.

Bentham's concern was not with the abolition of religion, but instead with segregating the use and funding of it from the public sphere to the private, minimising in the process the sinister interests of state, priests[1] and all those deriving such benefits from it in the public sphere. The aim was to place religion in the private sphere, to be funded by individuals - not the state - and to be partitioned from government decision-making. This corresponds with his empiricism, abolition of useless fictions[2] sinister interests,

---

[1] "From its birth to its death, the priest keeps his fixed eye on the prey he covers, and his prey is everything human that either breathes or has breathed ... No sooner are you born, than priestcraft lays hold of you, and
till you have paid toll to it, keeps shut against you the gate of the road which conducts you to your rights, and in return for the money, perhaps the 'uttermost farthing' thus exhorted from your friends, tell them that he has *christened* you; and unless this be done to you, and done by *him* to you, heaven, he informs them, has no comfort for you, nor will earth have any of which it is in his power to deprive you" (Fenn 1992:27).

[2] In the 1770s the law was obscure, absurd and composed with the prevalent use of legal fiction. Things were falsely described while straightforward falsehoods were accepted in court. Useless fictions were ones without
substance - no derivative or metaphysical / legal entity, such as natural law rights.

and the implementation of representative government[1] and not his alleged atheism.

This is one of the aspects which Crimmins (1990:304-5) fails to examine satisfactorily, interpreting Bentham's vision to include "a Utilitarian heaven on earth" and that the "secular Utilitarian society is one in which the State actively works to stamp out religion", where "a precondition for maximisation of utility is universal atheism". If this were true then the state would be acting coercively, thus being at odds with the notion that the duty of good government was to maximise the greatest happiness of the greatest number. An active program of "stamping" out religion may, *ceteris Paribus,* have led to a more rationally-geared society but at the inevitable cost of 'happiness', particularly amongst those possessing religious beliefs.[2]

Furthermore, it was the church's embodiment of religion which adversely manipulated men's minds by creating useless fictions and not religion per se.[3] Bentham may have shared some of the blame for not drawing a clear distinction between religion and the church. For example, in the *Temporal Happiness of Mankind* Bentham made a

---

[1] This is one which is democratic, following the utilitarian principle of maximising the greatest happiness of the greatest number.
[2] Another problem would be to transplant utilitarian morality in place of religious morality, something which may take many years and may lead to resentment, possibly even civil disobedience and/ or an assault on security.
[3] Bentham recognised that religion could be used as a useful fiction, particularly in its capacity of a sanction. An illustration of this can be seen in Bentham's theory of parliamentary sovereignty, where the sovereign was open to moral as well as religious censure by the public.

distinction between religion which was written (and from which the will of the deity could be discerned) and one which was not (he called the latter one 'natural' religion). His attack, while focusing on 'natural' religion, became vague due to the language subsequently adopted as the text proceeded, omitting the pre-fix 'natural'[1] (Beuchamp; 1822).

Part of the attack in the auto-icon pamphlet is, therefore, targeted towards the church as opposed to religion in general, for he saw this *institution* as illegitimate (amongst other things). Bentham's work, *Not Paul, but Jesus* can be interpreted as supporting this view. Even if one interprets Bentham as being anti-Christian, one cannot state that he was purely anti-religion, for he was predominantly influenced by the way religion was inter-woven and being manipulated and abused for self-gain by state and the church. In fact, it is a view which has contemporary analogous significance for those oppressed by dictators in so-called "Muslim states", for where government adopts the 'mask' of religion to shield itself from popular dissent (dissent here being tantamount to heresy) it is no longer representative. To this extent Bentham's endeavour to divorce religion from state action is commendable.

Another of Crimmin's assertions, that Bentham's goal was to construct a utilitarian society appears to be unsubstantiated, for while it is true that his work insisted upon the principle of utility it is difficult to see how one takes the leap from government applying utilitarian principles to maximise the greatest happiness of the

---

[1] It is not known how much of the omission of the prefix 'natural' is due to subsequent editing.

greatest number, with security being paramount, to a society totally ordered on utilitarian lines by a coercive legislator.

Meanwhile, the increased popularity of iconisation would have *cetris paribus* reduced the demand for burial services and thus driven down funeral charges. Moreover, increased supply of bodies for dissection would have led to economies of scale, with anatomists becoming more efficient in processing bodies and reducing as they did so the risk of black-marketeering in dead bodies, thus increasing public confidence. But it would have been the middle classes that would have gained the majority of the benefits of medical advances through the dissection of predominantly the indigent poor.

The indigent poor were aware of the disproportionate impact that the Anatomy Act would have had on them and consequently were not receptive to its provisions, and despite Bentham's apparently conservative reform proposals, it appears that in relation to the Act they were not conservative enough. But while he may be viewed as fairly conservative in his publicly held views on dissection, his proposals for an auto-icon which would be placed within a legislative framework reflects a political radicalism.

This is not surprising if one conceives Bentham's life to reflect a transformation to or perhaps even a return to political radicalism, the seeds of which can be found in Fragment on Government, where he launched an attack on one of the most influential English works on English common law, Blackstone's Commentaries on the Laws of England, making this a "lifetime's dialectic".[1]

While respecting Blackstone's endeavour at exposition of the English law (what is) Bentham considered this to be inferior to critical or 'censorial' jurisprudence as he called it (what ought to be).[2] It was the confusion resulting from the merging of these two which incensed Bentham, for attempting to justify the fictitious basis of common law could not be legitimate.

This was because the common law, according to Bentham, was inconsistent, incoherent, premised on and created useless fictions, reducing the population to abject subordination in order to further the sinister interests of what Bentham termed "Judge & Co". Moreover, common law created "Dog law"[3], leading to punishment on a retrospective basis and thus creating an offence which was not in existence at the time of the committed act.

Bentham objected to retrospective law-making of common law because such laws *defeated* expectations of the parties in the particular case at hand, thus seriously undermining security and consequently creating general alarm. The use

---

[1] See further, Burns (1989:23 40)

[2] Bentham claimed to espouse censorial jurisprudence. But it is difficult to see how he could create a clear distinction between the two. Bentham's work echoes both strands, although admittedly to differing degrees.

[3] "When your dog does anything you want to break him of, you wait till he does it, and then beat him for it. This is the way you make laws for your dog: and this is the way judges make laws for you and me. They won't tell a man beforehand what it is he *should not do* . . . they lie by till he has done something which they say he should not have done, and then they hang him for it" (Bowring v, 235).

of precedent produced mischief by perpetrating patterns and practices, rules and regulations more reflective of an earlier and probably different time, thus resulting in the paradox of inflexibility[1] (Postema; 1986:Ch.8). It is perhaps not surprising then that the auto-icon was proposed to be placed on a legislative footing.[2]

However, it may be argued that placing the auto-icon on a legislative footing was part of a long piece of satire on property law, for how could one take seriously property law which conceived of slaves as mere property, for such a conception would in theory have been in conflict with Bentham's interpretation of utilitarianism, which required everyone to be counted as one and no one as more than one, a concept which was not accepted, at least not in practice, in nineteenth century England, or for that matter, many other countries.

In fact, the auto-icon pamphlet is itself a predominantly satirical and sarcastic work, but an important one nevertheless in a number of respects. For example, it can be analogised as an index, not too dissimilar from those found in most books, pointing, in extremely summarised form, to the majority of Bentham's lifetime work, most of which had not been published by that time, and a large

---

[1] Precedent is premised upon certainty, so deviation from it, particularly in Bentham's time, would have undermined this. But if judges did not deviate from precedent the law was left reflecting outdated values or those present in a different time, thus reducing flexibility of the law to adapt to new situations effectively.

[2] "so various and so perplexing are the questions of property in reference to Auto-Iconism that it is humbly suggested to the influential and writing few to anticipate grievances, and provide remedies by an Auto-Icon statute law (Fenn 1992:20).

proportion of which remains to be edited and published today. The pamphlet is also important in the respect that it provides a more candid insight (but one which could only really be appreciated after reading Bentham's other works) of Bentham's personal thoughts and feelings on a range of issues.

Coupled with the fact that the pamphlet had been edited but not published leads one to re-enforce such a view, adding also that, in my view, Bentham may have intended it to be published once the time was right. What I mean by this is that it should be published when the works which are referred to in it (whether explicitly or implicitly) are also published. If this is correct then, bearing in mind that most of the related works have already been published, it is about time that it was published, with a commentary attached.

The final section, and one which is constrained by the length of my discussion, examines whether Bentham was an egoist and, if so, to what extent this prevailed upon his empirical approach. The aim of such examination is to assert that even if he was an egoist it should not devalue in any way his auto-icon or a well-researched interpretation of it.

4. Auto-iconism: empiricism or egoism?

While at a general level, egoism can be interpreted as being anything which brings an individual the greatest happiness, a specific interpretation reveals two distinct sub-categories contained within it: (a) psychological egoism, where everyone (as a matter of fact) always acts in their own interest; and (b) ethical egoism, where everyone *should* always act in their own best interest.

In analysing Bentham's insistence (at a practical level at least) that the proper end of good government should be to ensure the greatest happiness of the greatest number[1] - this being a normative stance - he does, however, recognise that governments do not (and nor do other institutions or individuals for that matter) adopt this position in reality. Accepting this interpretation identifies Bentham with the expositorial, as opposed to the censorial, conception of egoism (i.e. 'psychological' egoism)

Psychological egoism can be traced throughout Bentham's works, identifying institutions' and individuals' potential for incorporating sinister interest, particularly in the presence of a pecuniary motive. Adopting this conception, then, ensures an antithesis to idealism, something which was prevalent in the churches' interpretation of religion and the French Declaration's insistence upon non-legal rights. The difficulty that both these idealisms posed for society was that they had no identifiable 'anchoring' point[2], thus being vague and open to sinister interpretation and manipulation.

---

[1] His original formulation was for the greatest happiness of everyone. But
realising the impracticalities that this would generate he changed this to
the greatest happiness of the greatest number.
[2] An 'anchoring' point in relation to rights, according to Bentham, means a recognised legal duty which can be enforced at law by the claimant against the party in breach.

Moreover, Bentham maintained that for every motive (premised on pain or pleasure) there was a corresponding interest. He explained that "Of every human being the conduct is on every occasion at any moment determined by the conception which at that moment he has of his individual interest" (UC xviii 173). But as Dinwiddy (1990:23) notes "interest" for Bentham was not to be equated with 'self-interest' in the usual sense. For instance, while Bentham had divided motives into three main heads: social, dis-social and self-regarding[1], self-interest was not to be restricted to actions of a self-regarding nature but would have also been attributable to social or (semi)altruistic motives. Even (semi)altruistic motives were to further one's 'self-interest' to the extent of receiving gratification or happiness from doing so.

Viewing Bentham as possessing a psychological egoism compliments his empirical methodology, for in recognising the reality of institutions' and individuals' motives and behaviour reflects the frailties of human nature, providing a more coherent basis for developing safety mechanisms to overcome these (such as legal, moral and religious forms of censure, the Public Opinion Tribunal, open government and so forth).

If such an interpretation is accepted then the auto-icon-remains of Bentham reflect both his lifetime empiricism and egoism. 'Empiricism' incorporated his view that a body was merely a material thing (and so should not be treated as anything more because to do so would create a useless

---

[1] see diagram in appendix 1

fiction), as well as his rejection of church authority and its interpretation of Christianity[1], and his acceptance of the need for dissection to benefit the living. A more comprehensive account of 'egoism' is, however, difficult to construct, for, in the absence of explicit and authoritative material on Bentham's personal motivations, a psycho-analytical approach is required, something which is outside the parameters of this discussion. Bearing this in mind, one can only make a rudimentary evaluation of his egoistical nature.

For example, we know that Bentham left £2,000[2] to Bowring to edit and publish his manuscripts, thus potentially leading one to the conclusion that he wanted some form of recognition for his lifetime's work. In the absence of any progeny, there was no one to ensure *his* lineage and so this may have influenced his decision to be auto-iconised as a continual reminder to future generations of his existence, perhaps inspiring people to continue reading his work, something which it has facilitated directly - in relation to medical history and indirectly - in relation to academics running Bentham courses (at UCL in particular) , editing and publishing his manuscripts, as well as the increasing number of doctoral theses turned to books - emerging recently.

---

[1] In relation to the auto-icon its direct intention appears to have been to refute the 'sanctity' of the grave - a form of a "two-fingered" salute to the church and its influence on the establishment generally.
[2] This would equate to approximately £100,000 in today's financial terms - a figure which, given Bentham's voluminous and occasionally illegible work has required funding to run into seven figure sums for the Bentham Project at UCL (which is responsible for editing and publishing Bentham's remaining manuscripts) .

Bentham made it explicit in his will that " ... if it should so happen that my previous friends and other disciples should be disposed to meet together on some day or days of the year for the purpose of commemorating the founder of the greatest Happiness System of Morals and legislation my executor will from time to time cause to be conveyed to the room in which they meet the said box or case with the contents [of the Auto-Icon] there to be stationed in such part of the room as to the assembled company shall seem meet" (Fenn; 1992: 38). This is a rather peculiar request if viewed in isolation, but in combination with the auto-icon pamphlet it appears to be more than just egoism, continuing perhaps the general satirical trend.

My initial reaction to Bentham's auto-icon-remains was probably a common one, viewing it as a form of self-inflated egoism. But having located it within Bentham's wider legal and political thought this position, for me at least, can no longer be sustained. After all, I, like so many other individuals, desire recognition in one form or another for my contribution through either my labour for others (i.e. promotion and remuneration) or, if I were to write a book, for my creativity and analysis. Why then should we conceive Bentham's position as being significantly different from our own, particularly when the real difference is merely the medium for expressing egoism (i.e. his auto-icon-remains).

The auto-icon-remains and pamphlet represent a rather complex epitaph to a lifetime's commitment to empirically driven legal and political reform. If auto-iconism is egoism then what is burial? How different is a human auto-icon to a gravestone? The symbolic value of the two may possess different representations but the request from both is convergent. They both require respect and remembrance, although admittedly an auto-icon provides a more intense form of remembrance. Moreover, egoism is a part of human nature and to deny or exclude it completely is to deny its existence, and if Bentham were to do this it would contradict his broad empirically-driven approach.

Throughout Bentham's life he was cautious to dilute his radicalism by either not publishing his work or by publishing it under a pseudonym. Auto-iconism provides the equivalent of a 'two-fingered' salute to the establishment - the church. As for the auto-icon pamphlet there remains a degree of uncertainty as to whether Bentham intended to publish it or not. The fact that it was edited suggests that he anticipated its publication sometime in the future, probably when public opinion permitted. It is difficult to see any other reason to get such a piece of work edited by Bowring, who was to become responsible for a l so editing his other manuscripts after his death. Perhaps one could interpret it as an epitaph explaining the reason for the auto-icon-remains, and if this is so then it is effective, although not at first reading, and certainly not when read and analysed in isolation.

5. Conclusion

Rarely does a week pass at University College London without a guided tour of Bentham's auto-icon-remains, reminding us in the process of the paucity of people following his example since. Perhaps auto-iconism was another one of Bentham's proposals which was to be shelved, or merely a satirical attack on established orthodoxy; the possible interpretations are many.

Conversely, dissection has only had one interpretation in the West and that has been in terms of increased popularity, particularly in the latter half of this century, with post-mortems becoming commonplace and donation of organs for transplant being a persuasive moral argument for many.

While auto-iconism was promoted as reducing burial expenses, it would have incurred costs in itself and should therefore be viewed more in terms of a symbolic gesture against the power and influence of the church and an attack on irrational beliefs and taboos than a practical alternative. Dissection, on the other hand, encompassed more than mere symbolism or protestation it provided an encouragement to further medical science and methodology, one of Bentham's great loves (adopted from Newton, Bacon and the Enlightenment generally).

Bentham was not, however, alone in calling for society to accept dissection, but he added a unique philosophical, practical and completely committed dimension, which for his time was radical and commendable. His auto-icon remains, in relation to this at least, represents a reminder to us (particularly medical historians) of his unselfish contribution to the dissection debate, both in theory and in practice.

Appendix 1

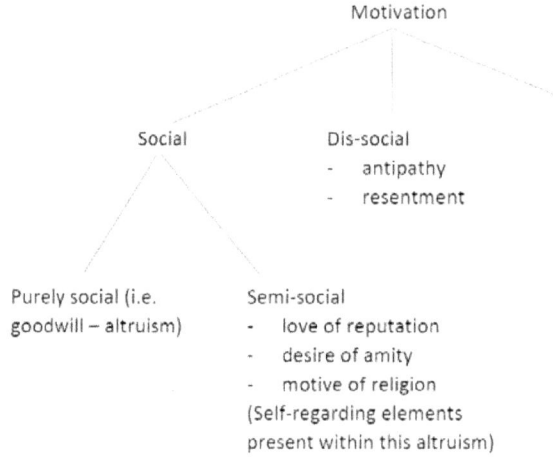

Motivation

Social   Dis-social
- antipathy
- resentment

Self-regarding
- physical desire
- pecuniary interest
- love of power
- self-preservation

Purely social (i.e.
goodwill – altruism)

Semi-social
- love of reputation
- desire of amity
- motive of religion
(Self-regarding elements
present within this altruism)

References and Bibliography

Beaucamp, Philip (1822): *Analysis of the Influence of Natural Religion on the Temporal Happiness of Mankind,* London

Berman, David (1990): *A History of Atheism in Britain: From Hobbes* to *Russell,* Routledge

Burns, J.H.: *Bentham and Blackstone: A Lifetime's Dialectic,* Utilitas Vol.1, 1989, 23-40

Dinwiddy, John (1990): *Bentham,* Past Masters, OUP

Fenn, Robert (1992): *Jeremy Bentham, Auto -Icon and the Last Will and Testament,* Torronto
First Principles preparatory to Constitutional Code, Collected Works

Hart, H.L.A. (1995): *An Introduction to the Principles of Morals and Legislation,* Publisher?

Kelly, Paul (1989): *Utilitarianism and Distributive Justice: The Civil Law and the Foundations of Bentham's Economic Thought,* Utilitas Vol.1

Postema (1986): *Bentham and the Common Law Tradition,* Clarendon Press Oxford

Quinn, Michael (May 1994): *Jeremy Bentham on the Relief of Indigence: an exercise in applied philosophy,* Utilitas Vol.6, No . 1

Richardson, Ruth: (1988) - *Death, Dissection and the Destitute,* Penguin Books
(1986) - *Bentham and "Bodies for Dissection",* Bentham Newsletter

Schofield, Philip: *The Constitutional Code of Jeremy Bentham,* Kings College Law Journal II (1991-2) 40-62

Smith, Gamaliel (1823): *Not Paul, but Jesus,* London

Waldron, J (1987): *Nonsense Upon Stilts,* Methuen

www.ingramcontent.com/pod-product-compliance
Lightning Source LLC
Chambersburg PA
CBHW072314200526
45168CB00014B/1506